T0198898

You've Got What It Takes!

By: Taryn Stark Wyant
Illustrations by: Tincho Shmidt

AuthorHouse™
1663 Liberty Drive
Bloomington, IN 47403
www.authorhouse.com
Phone: 1 (800) 839-8640

Because of the dynamic nature of the Internet, any web addresses or links contained in
this book may have changed since publication and may no longer be valid. The views
expressed in this work are solely those of the author and do not necessarily reflect the views
of the publisher, and the publisher hereby disclaims any responsibility for them.

This book is printed on acid-free paper.

ISBN: 978-1-7283-6517-6 (sc)
ISBN: 978-1-7283-6518-3 (e)
ISBN: 978-1-7283-6519-0 (hc)

Library of Congress Control Number: 2020911150

Print information available on the last page.

Published by AuthorHouse 06/23/2020

authorHOUSE®

In a land far away
where the dolphins swim free
there is a little girl
named Rosalee.

Rosalee loves to craft and to play
And to imagine grand kingdoms far, far away.

It was in a strange time
That our story begins.
When a sickness scared people
Showed his teeth when he grinned.

The sickness made people
Stay in their houses
With mommies and daddies,
Kitties and mouses.

Because people had to snuggle inside,
Many couldn't work for the food they would buy.
So Rosalee's friends all gathered together
To find food for their neighbors
So the storm they could weather.

They bought potatoes and milk and chocolate
breakfast bars. They packed them in boxes,
Then packed them in cars.
The cars all lined up
And the people looked thinner, till they gathered
their food to feed their families dinner.

Rosalee's friends
Helped out all the time,
They spent all their money,
But couldn't feed the whole line.

There were so many people in such great need
Of food and supplies,
So many mouths to feed!

And so Rosalee thought about how she could help,
Then had an idea
And called out with a "yelp!"

"What if I sold my drawings for money?
Then could we feed people bread, eggs, and honey?"

A brilliant idea!
Amazing! The best!
Her mommy and daddy got up
And got dressed

And pulled out the paper,
The crayons, and the easel.
Rosalee started drawing
To feed all the people!

In a short while,
The orders came in!
Rosalee drew pictures
With a wide, friendly grin.

She drew big elephants,
And piggies that snored!
She drew pretty rainbows
And the soft ocean shore.

She drew people and families
And kitties and views;
She may even have drawn
Someone just like you!

Over one thousand families
She was able to feed
In this time of scary sickness,
In this time of great need.

And Rosalee did it
Despite her sweet youth
She changed people's lives;
What a beautiful truth!

So let this remind you
If you're old and you're tall,
Or you're loud, or you're quiet,
Or you're young and quite small.

You've got what it takes
To change this great world
And make it even better
No matter what's unfurled.

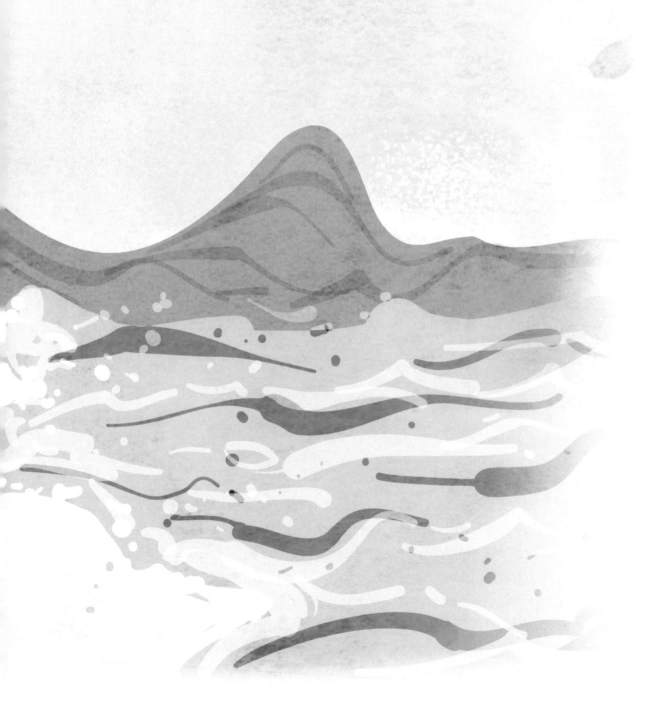

Rosalee Wyant was 3-years-old when the Coronavirus began having a worldwide impact. She lives in Lahaina, Maui with her family. The unemployment rate in Lahaina, Maui was the highest in the State of Hawaii, and one of the highest in the country, for the duration of the pandemic. In partnership with Lahaina Baptist Church, Rosalee became involved with the Lahaina Food Distribution, which spent months feeding over 600 families each week beginning in March 2020. Rosalee raised enough funds to feed over 1000 families through her philanthropy, "Drawings for Donations." A portion of the profits from her story, *You've Got What It Takes*, will go towards this continued cause until the need is met.

Printed in the United States
By Bookmasters